First World War
and Army of Occupation
War Diary
France, Belgium and Germany

66 DIVISION
Divisional Troops
Royal Army Veterinary Corps
1/1 East Lancashire Mobile Veterinary Section
1 March 1917 - 15 May 1919

WO95/3132/4

The Naval & Military Press Ltd
www.nmarchive.com
Published in association with The National Archives

Published by

The Naval & Military Press Ltd

Unit 10 Ridgewood Industrial Park,

Uckfield, East Sussex,

TN22 5QE England

Tel: +44 (0) 1825 749494

www.naval-military-press.com

www.nmarchive.com

This diary has been reprinted in facsimile from the original. Any imperfections are inevitably reproduced and the quality may fall short of modern type and cartographic standards.

© Crown Copyright
Images reproduced by permission of The National Archives, London, England, 2015.

Contents

Document type	Place/Title	Date From	Date To
Heading	WO95/3132/4		
Heading	66th Division 1-1st (EL) Mobile Vety Secn Mar 1917-May 1919		
Heading	War Diary of 1/1st East Lancs Mobile Veterinary Section From 1st March 1917 To 31st March 1917		
War Diary	Southampton	01/03/1917	01/03/1917
War Diary	Le Havre	02/03/1917	03/03/1917
War Diary	Berguette	04/03/1917	08/03/1917
War Diary	Guarbecque	09/03/1917	09/03/1917
War Diary	St Venant	10/03/1917	17/03/1917
War Diary	Bethune	18/03/1917	31/03/1917
Miscellaneous	D.A.G 3rd Echelon Base	30/04/1917	30/04/1917
Heading	War Diary of 1/1st East Lancs Mobile Veterinary Section From April 1st 1917 To April 30th 1917		
War Diary	Bethune	01/04/1917	30/04/1917
Miscellaneous	D.A.G 3rd Echelon Base	31/05/1917	31/05/1917
Heading	War Diary of the 1/1st East Lancs Mobile Vet. Section From 1st May 1917 To 31st May 1917 Vol 3		
War Diary	Bethune	01/05/1917	31/05/1917
Heading	War Diary of 1/1st East Lancs Mobile Veterinary Section From 1st June 1917 To 30th June 1917 Volume IV		
War Diary	Bethune Location Sheet 36.a E.11.c.2.6	01/06/1917	26/06/1917
War Diary	Lefarinckoucke Location Sheet 19 C.27.b.6.4	29/06/1917	30/06/1917
Heading	War Diary of 1/1 East Lancs Mobile Veterinary Section From 1st July 1917 To 31st July 1917 (Volume V)		
War Diary	Leffrinckoucke Location Sheet 19 C.2.9.a.2.8	02/07/1917	18/07/1917
War Diary	Coxydebains Location W.6.d.6.4 Map Coxyde 1/20000 Edition 1	19/07/1917	31/07/1917
Heading	War Diary of 1/1st East Lancs Mobile Veterinary Section From 1/8/17 To 31/8/17 (Volume 6)		
War Diary	Coxyde Bains Location W.6.d.6.4 Map Coxyde 1/20000 Edition 1	01/08/1917	31/08/1917
Heading	War Diary of 1/1 East Lancs Mobile Veterinary Section From 1st September 1917 To 30th September 1917 (Volume 7)		
War Diary	Coxyde Bains Location W.6.d.6.4 Map Coxyde 1/20000 Edition 1	01/09/1917	25/09/1917
War Diary	Leffrinckoucke Location C.29.a.2.8 Sheet 19	26/09/1917	26/09/1917
War Diary	Wemaers Cappel Location O.2.b.6.3 Sheet 27	27/09/1917	27/09/1917
War Diary	Arques Location S.10.c.80 Sheet 27	29/09/1917	30/09/1917
Heading	War Diary of 1/1st East Lancs Mobile Veterinary Section From 1st October 1917 To 31st October 1917 Volume VIII		
War Diary	Arques Location S.16.a.4.7 Sheet 27	01/10/1917	02/10/1917
War Diary	Eecke Location Q.13.c.12 Sheet 28	04/10/1917	04/10/1917
War Diary	St. Laurent Location F.18.b.9.8 Sheet 27	05/10/1917	06/10/1917
War Diary	Poperinge Location G.14.b.5.4 Sheet 28	08/10/1917	17/10/1917
War Diary	Wormhouldt Location I.6.d.2.4 Sheet 28	19/10/1917	19/10/1917
War Diary	Arques Location S.10.a.6.3 Sheet 27	22/10/1917	29/10/1917

Heading	War Diary of the 1/1st East Lancs Mobile Veterinary Section From 1st November To 30th November 1917 (Volume 9)		
War Diary	Arques Location S.10.a.b.3 Sheet 27	01/11/1917	01/11/1917
War Diary	Wallon Capelle	03/11/1917	09/11/1917
War Diary	Westhoutre	10/11/1917	12/11/1917
War Diary	Reninghelst	13/11/1917	16/11/1917
War Diary	Reninghelst Location G.28.d.5.2 Sheet 28	17/11/1917	24/11/1917
War Diary	Hazebrouck	28/11/1917	30/11/1917
Heading	War Diary of the 1/1 East Lancs Mobile Veterinary Section From 1st December 1917 To 31st December 1917 (Volume 10)		
War Diary	Hazebrouck Location V.28.c.4.0 Sheet 27	01/12/1917	15/12/1917
War Diary	St Marie Cappel Location P.27.a.4.8 Sheet 27	16/12/1917	28/12/1917
War Diary	Hondeghem Location U.6.a.9.8 Sheet 27	29/12/1917	31/12/1917
Heading	War Diary of the 1/1st East Lancashire Mobile Veterinary Section From 1st January 1918 To 31st January 1918 Volume XI		
War Diary	Hondeghem Location U.6.a.9.8 Sheet 27	01/01/1918	12/01/1918
War Diary	Reninghelst Location G.3.4.b.6.9 Sheet 28	13/01/1918	31/01/1918
Heading	War Diary of 1/1 East Lancs Mobile Veterinary Section From 1st Feby/1918 To 28th Feby/1918 Volume 12		
War Diary	Reninghelst Location G.34.b.6.9 Sheet 28	01/02/1918	10/02/1918
War Diary	Proven Location E.12.d.3.9	11/02/1918	18/02/1918
War Diary	Villers Bretonneux	19/02/1918	28/02/1918
Heading	War Diary of 1/1st East Lancashire Mobile Veterinary Section From 1st March/18 To 31/March/18 Volume XIII		
War Diary	Villers Brettoneaux 43 Rue D' Amiens	01/03/1918	01/03/1918
War Diary	Harbonniers	02/03/1918	02/03/1918
War Diary	Villers Carbonelles	03/03/1918	03/03/1918
War Diary	Vraignes Location Q.19.b.20	04/03/1918	16/03/1918
War Diary	Vraignes 43 Rue D' Amiens	17/03/1918	22/03/1918
War Diary	Doingt	23/03/1918	23/03/1918
War Diary	Biaches	24/03/1918	24/03/1918
War Diary	Cappy	25/03/1918	25/03/1918
War Diary	Mericourt	26/03/1918	26/03/1918
War Diary	Fouilloy	28/03/1918	28/03/1918
War Diary	Cagny	30/03/1918	30/03/1918
War Diary	Salouel	31/03/1918	31/03/1918
Heading	War Diary of the 1/1 East Lancs Mobile Veterinary Section From 1st April 1918 To 30th April 1918 (Volume 14)		
War Diary	Seux Amiens-17 2.b.3-7	01/04/1918	02/04/1918
War Diary	Long Abbeville-14 6.L.8.5	03/04/1918	04/04/1918
War Diary	Bellancourt Abbeville 5-k 9-1	05/04/1918	05/04/1918
War Diary	Oneux Abbeville 14 5L.7.7	06/04/1918	21/04/1918
War Diary	Long Abbeville 6.L.8.5	22/04/1918	22/04/1918
War Diary	Tilques Hazebrouck 57 C.3.5.4	24/04/1918	26/04/1918
War Diary	Val De Lumbres Hezebrouck 15a B.H.5.6	29/04/1918	30/04/1918
Heading	War Diary of 1/1st East Lancashire Mobile Veterinary Section From 1st May 1918 To 31st May 1918 Vol 15		
War Diary	Val De Lumbres	01/05/1918	01/05/1918
War Diary	Nielles Les Blequin	02/05/1918	02/05/1918
War Diary	Desvres	03/05/1918	03/05/1918
War Diary	Offeux	04/05/1918	31/05/1918

Heading	War Diary of the 1/1 East Lancs Mobile Veterinary Section From 1st June 1918 To 30th June 1918 (Volume 16)		
War Diary	Offeux	01/06/1918	21/06/1918
War Diary	Mesnil Trois Foetus	22/06/1918	22/06/1918
War Diary	Bernaville	24/06/1918	30/06/1918
Heading	War Diary of 1/1st East Lancashire Mobile Veterinary Section Volume 17 July 1918		
War Diary	Bernaville	02/07/1918	22/07/1918
War Diary	Gaillefontaine	23/07/1918	23/07/1918
War Diary	Abancourt	27/07/1918	27/07/1918
War Diary	Gaillefontaine	27/07/1918	31/07/1918
Heading	War Diary of the 1/1 East Lancs Mobile Veterinary Section From 1st August 1918 To 31st August 1918 (Volume 18)		
War Diary	Serques	01/08/1918	26/08/1918
Heading	War Diary of 1/1st East Lancs Mobile Veterinary Section From 1st Sept 1918 To 30th Sept 1918 Volume XIX		
War Diary	Serques	01/09/1918	16/09/1918
War Diary	Abancourt	17/09/1918	21/09/1918
War Diary	Lecauroy	23/09/1918	27/09/1918
War Diary	Raincheval	28/09/1918	28/09/1918
War Diary	Corbie	29/09/1918	29/09/1918
Heading	War Diary of 1/1st E Lancs M.V.S From 1st Oct/18 To 31st Oct/18 Volume XX		
War Diary	Morcourt	01/10/1918	01/10/1918
War Diary	Montauban	04/10/1918	04/10/1918
War Diary	Combles	05/10/1918	05/10/1918
War Diary	Ronssoy	07/10/1918	08/10/1918
War Diary	Beaurevoir	09/10/1918	09/10/1918
War Diary	Avelu	11/10/1918	12/10/1918
War Diary	Maretz	13/10/1918	20/10/1918
War Diary	Seraine	21/10/1918	31/10/1918
Heading	War Diary of the 1/1 East Lancs Mobile Veterinary Section From 1st November 1918 To 30th November 1918 (Volume 21)		
War Diary	Serain	01/11/1918	04/11/1918
War Diary	Le Cateau	05/11/1918	06/11/1918
War Diary	Landricies	07/11/1918	07/11/1918
War Diary	Taisnieres	10/11/1918	10/11/1918
War Diary	Dompierre	11/11/1918	12/11/1918
War Diary	Sars Poteries	13/11/1918	17/11/1918
War Diary	Solre Chateau	18/11/1918	18/11/1918
War Diary	Froid Chapelle	19/11/1918	19/11/1918
War Diary	Philipville	20/11/1918	24/11/1918
War Diary	Waulsort	03/12/1918	14/12/1918
War Diary	Ciney	15/12/1918	31/12/1918
Heading	War Diary of the 1/1 East Lancs Mobile Veterinary Section From 1st Dec 1918 To 31st Dec 1918 (Volume No.22)		
War Diary	Ciney	01/01/1919	31/01/1919
Heading	War Diary of the 1/1 East Lancs Mobile Veterinary Section From 1st Jany 1919 To 31st Jany 1919 (Volume 23)		

Heading	War Diary of 1st/1st East Lancs M.V.S 66th Division From 1st Feb 1919 To 28th Feb 1919 Volume XXIV		
War Diary	Ciney	01/02/1919	28/02/1919
Heading	War Diary of 1/1st East Lancashire Mobile Veterinary Section Volume 25 From 1-3-19 To 31-3-19		
Miscellaneous	Certificate Constatant L'Absence De Toute Maladie Contagieuse		
War Diary	Ciney	01/03/1919	31/03/1919
Heading	War Diary of 1/1st East Lancs Mobile Veterinary Section April 1919 Volume 26		
War Diary Miscellaneous	Ciney	01/04/1919	30/04/1919
Heading	War Diary of 1/1st East Lancs Mobile Veterinary Section Volume 27 May 1919		
War Diary	Ciney	05/05/1919	15/05/1919

WO 95/31324

66TH DIVISION

1-1ST (EL) MOBILE VETY SECN.

MAR 1917 - MAY 1919

Confidential

War Diary

of

1/1st East Lancs Mobile Veterinary Section

From 1st March 1917.

To 31st March 1917.

Army Form C. 2118.

WAR DIARY
or
INTELLIGENCE SUMMARY

(Erase heading not required.)

Instructions regarding War Diaries and Intelligence Summaries are contained in F. S. Regs., Part II. and the Staff Manual respectively. Title Pages will be prepared in manuscript.

Place	Date	Hour	Summary of Events and Information	Remarks and references to Appendices.
Southampton	1-3-17	4 p.m.	Embarked Officer 2/H6C/women 3 a.s.c. drivers 26 horses and 3 wagons (wheeled)	J.S.
Havre	2-3-17	9.30 am	Disembarked. Proceeded to Rest Camp	J.S.
—	3-3-17	5.29pm	Entrained for Bergeutte	J.S.
Bergeutte	4-3-17	6-op	Detrained and marched to Guarbeque. Collected 1 sick horse	J.S.
—	8-3-17		Shot 1 horse	J.S.
Guarbeque	9-3-17		Marched to St Venant	J.S.
St Venant	10-3-17		Collected 2 sick horses and admitted for treatment	J.S.
—	11-3-17		Sick horses admitted 6	J.S.
—	12-3-17		" " 10 (1 collected)	J.S.
—	13-3-17		" " 2 Died 1.	J.S.
—	15-3-17		" " 2 Collected 3 Lorries shovels loose collected	J.S.
—	16-3-17		" " 4	J.S.
—	17-3-17		Marched to Bethune Self inoc. admitted 5 Died 1	J.S.
Bethune	18-3-17		Self inoc. admitted 5 Evacuated 1.	J.S.
—	19-3-17		" " 5	J.S.
—	20-3-17		" " 12 Died 1	J.S.
—	21-3-17		" " 18 Destroyed 1, saved 1.	J.S.

continued :—

Army Form C. 2118.

* Continued :— II.

WAR DIARY
or
INTELLIGENCE SUMMARY

(Erase heading not required.)

Instructions regarding War Diaries and Intelligence Summaries are contained in F. S. Regs., Part II. and the Staff Manual respectively. Title Pages will be prepared in manuscript.

Place	Date	Hour	Summary of Events and Information	Remarks and references to Appendices
Pabbing	22-3-17		A.A. howitzer rounds 23. Issued 1. Evacuated 23	J.S.
	23-3-17		" " 8 " 3	J.S.
	24-3-17		" " 9 " 5 Destroyed 1, collected 6	J.S.
	25-3-17		" " 2 Evacuated 38	J.S.
	26-3-17		" " 1 Destroyed 1, used 1, Evacuated 8	J.S.
	27-3-17		" " 10 Iss'd 1 Issued 2	J.S.
	28-3-17		" " 1 Issued 1	J.S.
	29-3-17		" " 7 Issued 1	J.S.
	30-3-17		Ammunition orderlies Reford Park. 24 hours duty hand over to 6 Sub-section at Rolls Mr Howard	J.S.
	31-3-17		Iss'd nil, in hand 3. 5 Issued 1.	J.S.

30-4-17

In the Field

D.A.G.
3rd Echelon
Base

The enclosed War Diary for April are forwarded in accordance with G.R.O. 1598, if please

J. Shinwell Capt. A.V.C.
Commanding Mobile Veterinary Section,
1/1st East Lancs.

Confidential.

War Diary
of
1/1st East Lancs. Mobile Veterinary Section

From April 1st 1917 to April 30th 1917

Army Form C. 2118.

WAR DIARY
or
INTELLIGENCE SUMMARY

(Erase heading not required.)

Instructions regarding War Diaries and Intelligence Summaries are contained in F. S. Regs., Part II. and the Staff Manual respectively. Title Pages will be prepared in manuscript.

Place	Date	Hour	Summary of Events and Information	Remarks and references to Appendices
Bethune	1-4-17		4th Essex admitted 3 Evacuated 8 Issued 1 Horses clipped on Regt. Bath 220	J.S.
	2-4-17		" 7 " " Horses clipped 448	J.S.
	3-4-17		" 9 " 3 " Destroyed 1	J.S.
	4-4-17		" 2 Evacuated 18 Emals clipped 110.	J.S.
	5-4-17		" 9 Animals clipped 301	J.S.
	6-4-17		" 9 Issued 3 Animals clipped 481	J.S.
	7-4-17		" 8 Evacuated 25	J.S.
	8-4-17		" 2 Destroyed 1	J.S.
	9-4-17		" 2 Issued 1 Animals clipped 286	J.S.
	10-4-17		" 11 Animals clipped 437	J.S.
	11-4-17		" 5 Evacuated 13 Riding Bath used by 6th Division	J.S.
	12-4-17		" 5 Issued 1 " " " 6 "	J.S.
	13-4-17		" 9 Operations undertaken to with held to enable carrying to through the supports. After the Bath was opened it was found coming away from the bath being made of soft wood, the ends or sides had swelled out away & the bath being made of soft wood, the ends or sides were very considerably would at once. it was dangerous for horses to emerge therefrom.	J.S.

2449 Wt. W14957/M90 750,000 1/16 J.B.C. & A. Forms/C.2118/12.

WAR DIARY or INTELLIGENCE SUMMARY

Army Form C. 2118.

Place	Date	Hour	Summary of Events and Information	Remarks and references to Appendices
De Kure	Sept 14		Continued:- Thin water neely duly reported on A. F. a. 2118.	
	15		Sick Parades total 5 Paid 2	
	16		" 9 " 1 Evacuated 23	
	17		" 5 Issued 1	
	18		" 10 Discharged 1	
	19		" 14 " 1 Evacuated 32	
	20		" 7 Evacuated 8	
	21		" 11 Issued 2	
	22		" 6 " 1 Evacuated 16	
	23		" 5 Mustapol 1	
	24		" 21	
	25		" 13 Evacuated 07 Mus 1 Bull III 1	
	26		" 16 Collected 1	
	27		" 8 Roromitis 30 Issued 2 Sketye 1 5 Evacuated 20	
	28		" 6 Issued 2 Evacuated 6	
	29		" 8 " 5 " 15 Mustapol	
	30		" 4 " 1 " 8	
	31		" 6	

In the Field

D.A.G
3rd Echelon
Base

The enclosed War Diary for May
is forwarded in accordance with
GRO 1598 please

J. Spruell Capt V.O.
Commanding Mobile Veterinary Section
1/1 East Lancs. Div.

Confidential

War Diary of the
1/1st East Lancs Mobile Vet. Section

From 1st May 1917

To 31st May 1917

Army Form C. 2118.

WAR DIARY
or
INTELLIGENCE SUMMARY
(Erase heading not required.)

Instructions regarding War Diaries and Intelligence Summaries are contained in F. S. Regs., Part II. and the Staff Manual respectively. Title Pages will be prepared in manuscript.

4 EAST AFRICA MOBILE VETERINARY SECTION

Place	Date	Hour	Summary of Events and Information	Remarks and references to Appendices
Baltune	1-5-17		Sick horses admitted 6 Evacuated 11	J.S.
	2-5-17		" " " 4 Returned to Unit Reissued 1	J.S.
	3-5-17		" " " 6 Destroyed 1	J.S.
	4-5-17		" " " 8 Evacuated 17	J.S.
	5-5-17		" " " 1 Returned to Unit Reissued 1	J.S.
	6-5-17		" " " 1 " " " " 1 Destroyed 1	J.S.
	7-5-17		" " " 14 " " " " 1 Evacuated 2	J.S.
	8-5-17		" " " 6	J.S.
	9-5-17		" " " 6 Evacuated 19	J.S.
	10-5-17		" " " 8 Returned to Unit Reissued 1	J.S.
	11-5-17		" " " 2 Evacuated 4	J.S.
	12-5-17		" " " 3	J.S.
	13-5-17		" " " 4 Evacuated 7	J.S.
	14-5-17		" " " 6 6	J.S.
	15-5-17		" " " 4 Returned to Unit Reissued 2	J.S.

Army Form C. 2118.

WAR DIARY
or
INTELLIGENCE SUMMARY
(Erase heading not required.)

11 EAST LANCS.
MOBILE VETERINARY SECTION

Place	Date	Hour	Summary of Events and Information	Remarks and references to Appendices
Villers	16-5-17		Sick horses admitted 8. Evacuated 8. Destroyed 1	J.S.
	17-5-17		" " " " " " 1	J.S.
	18-5-17		" " " 4 Evacuated 5. Destroyed 1	J.S.
	19-5-17		" " " 7 Returned to Unit Messines 1	J.S.
	20-5-17		" " " 13 Destroyed 1 Horse – dipping bath repaired and used by 29th MVS	J.S.
	21-5-17		" " " 11 Evacuated 15. Died 1. Animals dipped 590 by 66" Division	J.S.
	22-5-17		" " " 2 Animals dipped 685 by 66" Division	J.S.
	23-5-17		" " " 5 Evacuated 6 Returned to Unit Messines 1. Dipping Bath used by 6" Division	J.S.
	24-5-17		" " " 4 Dipping Bath used by 39th MVS	J.S.
	25-5-17		" " " 3 Evacuated 10. Dipping Bath used by 6" Division	J.S.
	26-5-17		" " " 6 " 8 Owing to the rubber piping which conveils the water	J.S.
	27-5-17		to the unit having perished, the dipping bath could again not be used. Reported this to A.D.V.S.	J.S.
	28-5-17		" " " 1	J.S.
	29-5-17		" " " 2 Evacuated 7	J.S.
	30-5-17		" " " 2	J.S.
	31-5-17		" " " 8	J.S.

Vol 4

Confidential.

War Diary
of
1/1st East Lancs Mobile Veterinary Section.

from 1st June 1917 to 30th June 1917.

Volume IV.

Army Form C. 2118.

WAR DIARY
or
INTELLIGENCE SUMMARY

(Erase heading not required.)

Instructions regarding War Diaries and Intelligence Summaries are contained in F. S. Regs., Part II. and the Staff Manual respectively. Title Pages will be prepared in manuscript.

Place	Date	Hour	Summary of Events and Information	Remarks and references to Appendices
BETHUNE Sheet 36a. E II c 2.6	1-6-17		Sick Lines admitted 2. Evacuated 1.	J.S.
"	3-6-17		5 " 3	J.S.
"	4-6-17		11 Nil. 1	J.S.
"	5-6-17		Evacuated 10. Returned to Unit as cured 1.	J.S.
"	6-6-17		3 Returned to Unit as reviewed 5.	J.S.
"	7-6-17		7 " 1.	J.S.
"	2-6-17		4 Evacuated 13.	J.S.
"	9-6-17		3 "	J.S.
"	10-6-17		2 Returned to Unit as reviewed 1.	J.S.
"	11-6-17		4 " 1. Evacuated 5. Unstayed 1.	J.S.
"	12-6-17		4. Evacuated 1. Unstayed 1.	J.S.
"	13-6-17		1 "	J.S.
"	14-6-17		3 Returned to Unit as cured 1. Have dripping bath repaired and reived by 39 Adv. D.S.	J.S.

2449 Wt. W14957/M90 750,000 1/16 J.B.C. & A. Forms/C.2118/12.

Army Form C. 2118.

WAR DIARY
or
INTELLIGENCE SUMMARY
(Erase heading not required.)

II

Instructions regarding War Diaries and Intelligence Summaries are contained in F. S. Regs., Part II. and the Staff Manual respectively. Title Pages will be prepared in manuscript.

Place	Date	Hour	Summary of Events and Information	Remarks and references to Appendices
BETHUNE Location Sheet 36a E 11.c.2.6	15-6-17		Sick horses admitted 3. Animals clipped by 66th Division + 89.	J.S.
"	16-6-17		" " " 3. Evacuated 2.	J.S.
"	17-6-17		" " " 1. " 1. Destroyed 1	J.S.
"	18-6-17		" " " 7. Returned to Unit or cinisued 3. Destroyed 1. Owing to the iron sheeting separating from the side of the dipping bath, it could not again be used until replaced. This	J.S. J.S.
			was reported to A.R.V.S.	J.S.
"	19-6-17		Sick horses admitted 5. Returned to Unit or cinisued 2.	J.S.
"	20-6-17		" " " 3. " 1. Destroyed 1.	J.S. J.S.
"	21-6-17		" " " 2. Evacuated 16.	J.S.
"	22-6-17		" " " 3. Horse dipping bath repaired and used by 39th Div. V.S.	J.S.
"	23-6-17		" " " 5. Destroyed 1. Returned to Unit or cinisued 1. Dipping bath used by 39th M.V.S.	J.S.
"	24-6-17		Two horses returned to Unit or cinisued	J.S.
"	25-6-17		Twelve horses evacuated	J.S.

Army Form C. 2118.

WAR DIARY
or
INTELLIGENCE SUMMARY

(Erase heading not required.)

Instructions regarding War Diaries and Intelligence Summaries are contained in F. S. Regs., Part II. and the Staff Manual respectively. Title Pages will be prepared in manuscript.

III

Place	Date	Hour	Summary of Events and Information	Remarks and references to Appendices
BETHUNE Location Sheet 36 n E n c 2.d	26-6-17		One hour transferred to 35th dir. U.S. Left BETHUNE 9.30 am. Entrained FOURUERIUL 10.30 am. arrived	J.S.
			DUNKERQUE 5.30 pm detrained and marched to PONT de LEFFRINCKOUCKE and arrived 9.15 pm.	J.S.
			Location Sheet 19 C 27 b 6.4	J.S.
LEFFRINCKOUCKE Location Sheet 19 C 27 b 6.4	27-6-17		One strayed mule admitted	J.S.
	30-6-17		Marched to farm Location sheet 19 C 29 a.2.2	J.S.

Russell Capt
Commanding Mobile Vety Sec
1/1 East Lancs

2449 Wt. W14957/M90 750,000 1/16 J.B.C. & A. Forms/C.2118/12.

Confidential.

War Diary

of.

1/1 East Lancs Mobile Veterinary Section.

From 1st July 1917   To:- 31st July 1917.

(Volume V.)

Army Form C. 2118.

WAR DIARY
or
INTELLIGENCE SUMMARY

(Erase heading not required.)

Instructions regarding War Diaries and Intelligence Summaries are contained in F. S. Regs., Part II. and the Staff Manual respectively. Title Pages will be prepared in manuscript.

Place	Date	Hour	Summary of Events and Information	Remarks and references to Appendices
LEFFRINCKOUCKE Location Sheet 19 C 29 a 2 8	3-7-17		Sick horses admitted 11.	J.S.
"	4-7-17		2. Returned to Unit or reissued 1.	J.S.
"	6-7-17		3. Evacuated 13.	J.S.
"	7-7-17		1. War establishment increased to 25 O.R. Authority O.4c. Base Records 12/824/17 dated 3-7-17.	J.S.
"	8-7-17		1.	J.S.
"	9-7-17		1.	J.S.
"	10-7-17		1.	J.S.
"	11-7-17		1.	J.S.
"	12-7-17		2.	J.S.
"	13-7-17		2. Returned to Unit or reissued.	J.S.
"	14-7-17		2.	J.S.
"	15-7-17		1.	J.S.
"	16-7-17		2. Destroyed 2.	J.S.
"	17-7-17		3. Evacuated 5. Destroyed 2. Returned to Unit or reissued 1.	J.S.
"	18-7-17		1. Left LEFFRINCKOUCKE 9.30 a.m. and marched to Coxyde Bains, and arrived 2-0 p.m. Location Wed 6.4. Map Coxyde Hazoux Edition 1. COXYDE BAINS	J.S.

Army Form C. 2118.

WAR DIARY
or
INTELLIGENCE SUMMARY
(Erase heading not required.)

Instructions regarding War Diaries and Intelligence Summaries are contained in F. S. Regs., Part II. and the Staff Manual respectively. Title Pages will be prepared in manuscript.

Place	Date	Hour	Summary of Events and Information	Remarks and references to Appendices
COXYDE BAINS Location w/e 6.11 Obs of COXYDE (page) & children i	19-7-17		Sick horses admitted 1. Returned to Unit or received 3. No: 509 S/Sergt Sweetman J.S. joined for duty.	J.S.
"	20-7-17	"	6.	J.S.
"	21-7-17	"	5. Returned to Unit or received 4. Died 1.	J.S.
"	22-7-17	"	9.	J.S.
"	23-7-17	"	5. Returned to Unit or received 2.	J.S.
"	24-7-17	"	2. Evacuated 16.	J.S.
"	25-7-17	"	4.	J.S.
"	26-7-17	"	4.	J.S.
"	27-7-17	"	1. Returned to Unit or received 2.	J.S.
"	28-7-17	"	7.	J.S.
"	29-7-17	"	4. Returned to Unit or received 1.	J.S.
"	30-7-17	"	3.	J.S.
"	31-7-17	"	9. Evacuated 19. Returned to Unit or received 1.	J.S.

J. Spruell Capt. A.V.C.
Commanding Mobile Veterinary Section,
1/1 East Lancs.

Vol 6

Confidential

War Diary
of
1/1st East Lancs Mobile Veterinary Section

From 1/8/17   To 31/8/17

(Volume 6)

Army Form C. 2118.

WAR DIARY
or
INTELLIGENCE SUMMARY

(Erase heading not required.)

Instructions regarding War Diaries and Intelligence Summaries are contained in F. S. Regs., Part II. and the Staff Manual respectively. Title Pages will be prepared in manuscript.

Place	Date	Hour	Summary of Events and Information	Remarks and references to Appendices
COXYDE BAINS Location W&d 6.4 Map COXYDE 1/20000 Edition 1.	1-8-17		Sick horses admitted 5.	J.S.
"	2-8-17		2.	J.S.
"	3-8-17		2. Returned to Unit or removed 1.	J.S.
"	4-8-17		" " 2.	J.S.
"	5-8-17		5. Destroyed 1.	J.S.
"	6-8-17		5. Died 1.	J.S.
"	7-8-17		2. Returned to Unit or removed 1. Evacuated 27.	J.S.
"	8-8-17		4.	J.S.
"	9-8-17		1.	J.S.
"	10-8-17		1. Destroyed 2. Returned to Unit or removed 2.	J.S.
"	11-8-17		3.	J.S.
"	12-8-17		7.	J.S.
"	13-8-17		6. Returned to Unit or removed 1. Destroyed 1.	J.S.
"	14-8-17		2. Evacuated 18.	J.S.
"	15-8-17		1.	J.S.

Army Form C. 2118.

WAR DIARY
or
INTELLIGENCE SUMMARY

(Erase heading not required.)

Instructions regarding War Diaries and Intelligence Summaries are contained in F. S. Regs., Part II. and the Staff Manual respectively. Title Pages will be prepared in manuscript.

Place	Date	Hour	Summary of Events and Information	Remarks and references to Appendices
CONDE BAINS Station N 6 d 4 h Map CONDE 57c.ov 1 2 a & d 2	17-8-17		Sick horses admitted 5. Returned to Unit or reissued.	J.S.
	18-8-17		" 9. Died 1.	J.S.
	19-8-17		" 16. Died 1.	J.S.
	20-8-17		" 2. Died 1 Returned to Unit or reissued 1.	J.S.
	21-8-17		" " Evacuated 33.	J.S.
	22-8-17		" 2. Returned to Unit or reissued 2.	J.S.
	23-8-17		" 2. Died 1.	J.S.
	24-8-17		" 5. Returned to Unit or reissued 2.	J.S.
	25-8-17		" 4. Died 1.	J.S.
	"		" 19.	J.S.
	26-8-17		" 4. Died 1 Returned to Unit or reissued 3	J.S.
	27-8-17		" 2. Evacuated 35.	J.S.
	29-8-17		" 4.	J.S.
	30-8-17		" 1.	J.S.
	31-8-17			J.S.

J. Purcell Capt: S. V.C.
Commanding Mobile Vety Section,
1/ East Lancs.

CONFIDENTIAL.

War Diary
of
1/1 East Lancs Mobile Veterinary Section

From 1st September 1917   To 30th September 1917.

(Volume 7)

Army Form C. 2118.

WAR DIARY
or
INTELLIGENCE SUMMARY

(Erase heading not required.)

Instructions regarding War Diaries and Intelligence Summaries are contained in F. S. Regs., Part II. and the Staff Manual respectively. Title Pages will be prepared in manuscript.

Place	Date	Hour	Summary of Events and Information	Remarks and references to Appendices
CONDE BAINS Location W.6.d.6.4 1/1 F.A. CONDE BAINS Sheet 1 London 1	1-9-17		Sick Parade admitted 14. destroyed 1.	J.S.
"	2-9-17		18.	J.S.
"	3-9-17			J.S.
"	4-9-17		6. died 1.	J.S.
"	5-9-17		Evacuated 37. died 1.	J.S.
"	6-9-17		5. destroyed 1.	J.S.
"	7-9-17		3.	J.S.
"	8-9-17		3.	J.S.
"	9-9-17		6. Returned to Unit in reserve 4.	J.S.
"	10-9-17		18.	J.S.
"	11-9-17		destroyed 4.	J.S.
"	12-9-17		Evacuated 25.	J.S.
"	13-9-17		Returned to Unit in reserve 3.	J.S.
"	14-9-17		4.	J.S.
"	15-9-17		13 died 2	J.S.
"	16-9-17		1. Returned to Unit as occomed 1.	J.S.
"	17-9-17		2. Evacuated 22.	J.S.
"	18-9-17		3.	J.S.
"	19-9-17		Returned to Unit as missing 2.	J.S.
"	20-9-17			J.S.

Army Form C. 2118.

WAR DIARY
or
INTELLIGENCE SUMMARY
(Erase heading not required.)

Instructions regarding War Diaries and Intelligence Summaries are contained in F. S. Regs., Part II. and the Staff Manual respectively. Title Pages will be prepared in manuscript.

Place	Date	Hour	Summary of Events and Information	Remarks and references to Appendices
COXYDE BAINS Location W6d 6.4 Sheet COXYDE Proper 23.9.17 Edition 1	21-9-17		Sick horses admitted 4. Died 1.	J.S.
			30.	J.S.
	24-9-17		4. Died 1. Returned to Unit or issued 1.	J.S. J.S.
	25-9-17		Evacuated 42. Left COXYDE BAINS 11.45 p.m. and marched to	J.S. J.S.
LEFFRINCKOUCKE Location C 29 a 2.8. Sheet 19	26-9-17		LEFFRINCKOUCKE and arrived 9.45 a.m. Location Sheet 19. C 29 a 2.8.	J.S.
			Left LEFFRINCKOUCKE 8-15 a.m., marched to GHYVELDE. Location Sheet 19. D 21. b 8.2. and arrived 9-30 a.m. Met 197 Infantry Brigade Transport and left GHYVELDE 10-a a.m. and marched to WEMAERS-CAPPEL and arrived 3-0 p.m. Location O 2 b 6.3. Sheet 27.	J.S. J.S. J.S. J.S.
WEMAERS CAPPEL O 2. b.6.3. Sheet 27 Location	27-9-17		Left WEMAERS CAPPEL 8-30 a.m. and marched to ARQUES. and arrived 1-30 p.m. Location S 10. c 8.0. Sheet 27	J.S. J.S.
ARQUES Location S.10.c.30. Sheet 27	29-9-17		Sick horses admitted 1.	J.S.
	30-9-17		3.	J.S.

J. Freel Capt. A.V.C.
Commanding 161th Veterinary Section.

2449 Wt. W14957/M90 750,000 1/16 J.B.C. & A. Forms/C.2118/12.

War Diary

of

1/1st East Lancs. Mobile Veterinary Section.

From 1st October 1917.   To: 31st October 1917.

Volume VIII.

Army Form C. 2118.

WAR DIARY
or
INTELLIGENCE SUMMARY

(Erase heading not required.)

Instructions regarding War Diaries and Intelligence Summaries are contained in F. S. Regs., Part II. and the Staff Manual respectively. Title Pages will be prepared in manuscript.

Place	Date	Hour	Summary of Events and Information	Remarks and references to Appendices
ARQUES Location S.16.a.u.7. Sheet 27	1-10-17		Sick horses admitted 3. Evacuated 6. Returned to Unit or assessed 1.	J.S.
	2-10-17		" 1. Left ARQUES, location S.16.a.u.7. Sheet 28 at 9-0 am and marched to EECKE, location B.13.c.12. Sheet 28, arrived 2-0 pm.	J.S.
EECKE Location B.13.c.12. Sheet 28	4-10-17		Left EECKE 10-0 pm and marched to ST LAURENT, location J.18.6.9.8. Sheet 29, arrived 2-0 am.	J.S.
		1-0 pm	Sick horses admitted 16.	J.S.
ST LAURENT Location J.18.6.9.8. Sheet 27	5-10-17		Sick horses admitted 1.	J.S.
	6-10-17	10-0 am	Sick horses evacuated 15. Left ST LAURENT, location J.18.6.9.8. Sheet 27, and marched to POPERINGE, location J.14.b.5.H. Sheet 28, arrived 5-0 pm.	J.S.
POPERINGE Location J.14.b.5.H. Sheet 28	8-10-17		Sick horses admitted 6.	J.S.
	9-10-17		" Returned to Unit or assessed 1.	J.S.
	10-10-17		" 5 Evacuated 4.	J.S.
	11-10-17		" 24. Evacuated 22.	J.S.
	12-10-17		" 4 Evacuated 9.	J.S.
	13-10-17		" 6 Evacuated 3.	J.S.
	15-10-17		" 11. Evacuated 1.	J.S.

2449 Wt. W14957/M90 750,000 1/16 J.B.C. & A. Forms/C.2118/12.

Army Form C. 2118.

WAR DIARY
or
INTELLIGENCE SUMMARY

(Erase heading not required.)

Instructions regarding War Diaries and Intelligence Summaries are contained in F. S. Regs., Part II. and the Staff Manual respectively. Title Pages will be prepared in manuscript.

Place	Date	Hour	Summary of Events and Information	Remarks and references to Appendices
POPERINGE Location G.14 d 5.4 (sheet 28)	16-10-17		Sick horses admitted 20. Evacuated 5. Destroyed 1.	J.S.
"	17-10-17		" " " 2. Evacuated 3H. Left POPERINGE, location G.14 d 5.4, sheet 28, 1·15 pm and	J.S.
"			marched to WORMHOUDT, location I.6 d.2.4, arrived 6·30 pm.	J.S.
WORMHOUDT Location I.6 d 2 H (sheet 8) ARQUES Location S.10 a 6.3 (sheet 27)	19-10-17		Left WORMHOUDT 9·15 am. and marched to ARQUES, location S.10 a 6.3, sheet 27, arrived 4·30 pm.	J.S.
"	22-10-17		Sick horses admitted 6	J.S.
"	23-10-17		" " " 4. Returned to Unit 1 evacuated 1.	J.S.
"	24-10-17		" " Evacuated 9.	J.S.
"	25-10-17		" " admitted 3	HJ.
"	28-10-17		" " " 2	HJ.
"	29-10-17		" " 3. Evacuated 4.	HJ.

H. Friend
Lieut. AVC
for OC Commanding A. VS
2nd/1 East Lancs

WAR DIARY

of the

1/1ST East Lancs Mobile Veterinary Section

From 1st November to 30th November 1917.

(Volume 9)

Army Form C. 2118.

WAR DIARY
INTELLIGENCE SUMMARY.
(Erase heading not required.)

Instructions regarding War Diaries and Intelligence Summaries are contained in F. S. Regs., Part II. and the Staff Manual respectively. Title pages will be prepared in manuscript.

Place	Date	Hour	Summary of Events and Information	Remarks and references to Appendices
ARQUES Location 51 Q A.6.3 Sheet 27	1-11-17		Left ARQUES 11-0 am and marched to WALLON CAPELLE, arrived 3.30 pm. Location U 24 c.2.5. Sheet 27	J.S.
"	"		Sick animals evacuated 3	J.S.
WALLON CAPELLE 3-11-17			Sick animals admitted 20.	J.S.
"	4-11-17		" " " 2. Evacuated 21.	J.S.
"	5-11-17		" " " 46	J.S.
"	6-11-17		" " evacuated 45.	J.S.
"	7-11-17		" " admitted 45 Evacuated 3	J.S.
"	8-11-17		" " " 8 do 52	J.S.
"	9-11-17		Left WALLON CAPELLE 9-30 am, marched to WESTHOUTRE, and arrived 4-30 pm. Location M.9.c.2.2. Sheet 27	J.S.
WESTHOUTRE	10-11-17		Sick horses admitted 1	J.S.
"	12-11-17		Left WESTOUTRE 10-30 am, marched to RENINGHLST, arrived 12-0 pm. Location J.22.d.5.2. Sheet 28	J.S.
RENINGHLST	"		Sick animals admitted 13	J.S.
"	13-11-17		" " " 8	J.S.
"	14-11-17		" " " 3. Evacuated 3. Destroyed 1. Returned & returned to Unit 1.	J.S.
"	15-11-17		" " " 17 Evacuated 1.	J.S.
"	16-11-17		" " " 16. Evacuated 1.	J.S.

Army Form C. 2118.

WAR DIARY
INTELLIGENCE SUMMARY.
(Erase heading not required.)

Instructions regarding War Diaries and Intelligence Summaries are contained in F. S. Regs., Part II. and the Staff Manual respectively. Title pages will be prepared in manuscript.

Place	Date	Hour	Summary of Events and Information	Remarks and references to Appendices
RENINGHLST Location G.28.d.5.2. Sheet 28	17-11-17		Sick animals admitted 13. Evacuated 1. Died 1.	J.S.
"	18-11-17		" " " 13. do 42.	J.S. J.S.
"	19-11-17		" " " 15. do 2.	J.S. J.S.
"	20-11-17		" " " 5.	J.S.
"	21-11-17		" " " 11.	J.S.
"	22-11-17		" " " 14. Evacuated 21. Received & returned to Unit 1.	J.S.
"	23-11-17		" " " 10. do 65	J.S.
"	24-11-17		Left RENINGHLST 9.30 am, marched to HAZEBROUCK, arrived 3.0 pm. Location V.2.8.c.H.O. Sheet 27	J.S.
HAZEBROUCK	28-11-17		Sick animals admitted 3.	J.S.
"	29-11-17		" " " 1	J.S.
"	30-11-17		" " " 22	J.S.

J. Sewell Capt. A.V.C.
Commanding Mobile Veterinary Section,
1/(East Lancs.)

WAR DIARY.

of the

1/1 East Lancs Mobile Veterinary Section

From 1st December 1917   to   31st December 1917.

(Volume 10).

Army Form C. 2118.

WAR DIARY
INTELLIGENCE SUMMARY.
(Erase heading not required.)

Instructions regarding War Diaries and Intelligence Summaries are contained in F. S. Regs., Part II. and the Staff Manual respectively. Title pages will be prepared in manuscript.

Place	Date	Hour	Summary of Events and Information	Remarks and references to Appendices
HAZEBROUCK Location V.28 c. H.Q. Sheet 27	1-12-17		Sick horses admitted 7. Evacuated 23	J.S.
"	2-12-17		" " " 3. " 7	J.S.
"	3-12-17		" " " 1. " 3	J.S.
"	4-12-17		" " " 7. " 3	J.S.
"	5-12-17		" " " 2. " 8	J.S.
"	6-12-17		" " " 23. " 2	J.S.
"	7-12-17		" " " 2. " 24	J.S.
"	8-12-17		" " " 16. Died 1.	J.S.
"	9-12-17		" " " 3. Evacuated 20	J.S.
"	10-12-17		" " " 2. "	J.S.
"	11-12-17		" " evacuated 1	J.S.
"	12-12-17		" " admitted 15 Evacuated 11	J.S.
"	13-12-17		" " " 2	J.S.
"	14-12-17		" " " 2	J.S.
"	15-12-17		Left HAZEBROUCK 8-30 A.M. marched to ST. MARIE CAPPEL, and arrived 10-45 A.M. Location P.27 a.4.8. Sheet 27.	J.S.

WAR DIARY or INTELLIGENCE SUMMARY.

Army Form C. 2118.

Place	Date	Hour	Summary of Events and Information	Remarks and references to Appendices
ST. MARIE CAPPEL P.27.a.4.8. Sheet 27	16-12-17		Sick horses admitted 8. Evacuated 1	G.S.
"	17-12-17		do 6	G.S.
"	18-12-17		" 12	G.S.
"	19-12-17		" 4 " 11	G.S.
"	20-12-17		" 7 " 5. Astrayed 1.	G.S.
"	21-12-17		" 4. 11 O.R. Category A despatched to No other Category "A" men.	G.S.
"	22-12-17		" 1 Evacuated 10.	G.S.
"	23-12-17		" 2. 10 O.R. Category A men despatched to No 2 Veterinary Hospital	G.S.
"	24-12-17		" 1 1 O.R. arrived from No 2 Veterinary Hospital	G.S.
"	25-12-17		" 4. 1 O.R. Category A man despatched to No. Veterinary Hospital	G.S.
"	28-12-17		" 4. Left ST. MARIE CAPPEL 11-0 a.m. marched to HONDEGHEM, and arrived	G.S.
HONDEGHEM Location U.6.a.9.8. Sheet 27			at 12-0 noon. Location U.6.a.9.8. Sheet 27.	
"	29-12-17		Sick horses admitted 2. Evacuated 4.	G.S.
"	30-12-17		" " 1	G.S.
"	31-12-17		" " 5	G.S.

J. Burrell Capt.

Confidential

War Diary

of the

1/1st East Lancashire Mobile Veterinary Section

From: 1st January 1918.   To: 31st January 1918.

Volume XI.

Army Form C. 2118.

WAR DIARY
or
INTELLIGENCE SUMMARY.
(Erase heading not required.)

Instructions regarding War Diaries and Intelligence Summaries are contained in F. S. Regs., Part II. and the Staff Manual respectively. Title pages will be prepared in manuscript.

Place	Date	Hour	Summary of Events and Information	Remarks and references to Appendices
HONDEGHEM Location U6a 9.8 Sheet 27	1-1-18		Sick animals admitted 3 Evacuated 1	J.S.
"	2-1-18		" " " 1 " "	J.S.
"	3-1-18		" " " 1 " "	J.S.
"	4-1-18		" " " 3 " "	J.S.
"	5-1-18		" " " " Evacuated 11	J.S.
"	7-1-18		" " " 5 " "	J.S.
"	8-1-18		" " " 7 Evacuated 8	J.S.
"	9-1-18		" " " 1 do 7	J.S.
"	10-1-18		" " " 7 " "	J.S.
"	11-1-18		" " " 4 Evacuated 8	J.S.
"	12-1-18		" " " 18 do 4. Left HONDGHEM 9-0 A.M. and marched to	J.S.
RENINGHLST Location G.3.4 b 6.9 Sheet 28	13-1-18		RENINGHLST. arrived at 2-0 p.m. Location G 3.4 b 6.9 Sheet 28. Sick Animals admitted 13	J.S.
"	14-1-18		" " " 5. Received & returned to Unit 1.	J.S.
"	15-1-18		" " " 4 Evacuated 1 Destroyed 1	J.S.
"	16-1-18		" " " 7 " "	J.S.

Army Form C. 2118.

WAR DIARY
INTELLIGENCE SUMMARY.
(Erase heading not required.)

Place	Date	Hour	Summary of Events and Information	Remarks and references to Appendices
RENINGHELST Location 9.34 b.6.9. Sheet 28	17-1-18		Sick animals admitted 11. Received & returned to Unit 1. Evacuated 35.	J.S.
"	18-1-18		" " " 15.	J.S.
"	19-1-18		" " " 7. Evacuated 1.	J.S.
"	20-1-18		" " " 1. " 1. Received & returned to Unit 1. Destroyed 1.	J.S.
"	21-1-18		" " " 11. " 2.	J.S.
"	22-1-18		" " " 9. " 1.	J.S.
"	23-1-18		" " " 11. Evacuated 49.	J.S.
"	24-1-18		" " " 3.	J.S.
"	25-1-18		" " " 12. Received & returned to Unit 1.	J.S.
"	26-1-18		" " " 1.	J.S.
"	27-1-18		" " " 27. Evacuated 2.	J.S.
"	29-1-18		" " " 7. " 1. Received & returned to Unit 1.	J.S.
"	31-1-18		" " " 12. " 50.	J.S.

J. Purcell Capt A.V.C.
Commanding Mobile Veterinary Section,
1/1 East Lancs.

Confidential

War Diary

of

1/1 East Lancs Mobile Veterinary Section

From 1st Feby/1918
to 28th Feby/1918

Volume 12

WAR DIARY
or
INTELLIGENCE SUMMARY.

(Erase heading not required.)

Army Form C. 2118.

Place	Date	Hour	Summary of Events and Information	Remarks and references to Appendices
RENINGHLST Location g 34 b 6.9 Shut 28	1.2.18		Sick horses admitted 1. Received & returned to Unit 2.	J.S.
"	2.2.18		" " " 2	J.S.
"	3.2.18		" " 11 Received & returned to Unit 1.	J.S.
"	4.2.18		" " 13 5 Destroyed one	J.S.
"	5.2.18		" " 55 3	J.S.
"	6.2.18		" " 2	J.S.
"	7.2.18		" " 1 Evacuated 93	J.S.
"	8.2.18		" " 1 2	J.S.
"	9.2.18		" " 1 Evacuated 3	J.S.
"	10.2.18		Received & returned to Unit 1. Left RENINGHLST 10·0 am and marched to	J.S.
PROVEN Location E.12.d.39	11.2.18		PROVEN arrived 1·0 p.m. Location E.12.d.39 Sheet 27	J.S.
"	12.2.18		Sick animals admitted 2.	J.S.
"	13.2.18		" " 6	J.S.
"	14.2.18		" " 53 5 Evacuated 7, Received & returned to Unit 1	J.S.
"	15.2.18		" " 1 6	J.S.
"	16.2.18		" " 54	J.S.

Army Form C. 2118.

WAR DIARY
or
INTELLIGENCE SUMMARY.
(Erase heading not required.)

Instructions regarding War Diaries and Intelligence Summaries are contained in F. S. Regs., Part II. and the Staff Manual respectively. Title pages will be prepared in manuscript.

Place	Date	Hour	Summary of Events and Information	Remarks and references to Appendices
PROVEN Location E.12 d.S.9 Sheet 27	17-2-18		Sick knees in hospital 1.	J.S.
	18-2-18		Left PROVEN 12-30am. marched to PROVEN RAILHEAD. Entrained 2-30 A.M. and left at 3-30 A.M. arrived GUILLECOURT 6-30 p.m. Detrained and marched to VILLERS BRETONNEUX, arrived 9-30 p.m.	J.S.
			Location. #3 Rue d'Amiens. Sheet Amiens 62 17.	J.S.
VILLERS BRETONNEUX	19-2-18		Sick knees admitted 2	J.S.
	20-2-18		14	J.S.
	21-2-18		1	J.S.
	22-2-18		9	J.S.
	23-2-18		9 Evacuated 24	J.S.
	24-2-18		1	J.S.
	25-2-18		28	J.S.
	26-2-18		3 Evacuated 41	J.S.
	27-2-18		3	J.S.
	28-2-18		3	J.S.

J. Snell Capt. V.S.
Commanding Mobile Vety Sectn
4. East Lancs.

Confidential

War Diary

of

1/1st East Lancashire Mobile Veterinary Section.

From 1st March/18.   To. 31/March/18.

Volume XIII

Army Form C. 2118.

WAR DIARY
INTELLIGENCE SUMMARY.

(Erase heading not required.)

Instructions regarding War Diaries and Intelligence Summaries are contained in F. S. Regs., Part II. and the Staff Manual respectively. Title pages will be prepared in manuscript.

Place	Date	Hour	Summary of Events and Information	Remarks and references to Appendices
VILLERS BRETONNEAUX 43 Rue d'Amiens	1-3-18		Left VILLERS BRETONNEAUX 1-15 pm, marched to HARBONNIERS and arrived 3-15 pm.	J.S.
HARBONNIERS	2-3-18		Sick animals evacuated 10. Left HARBONNIERS 9-0 a.m. marched to VILLERS CARBONELLES and arrived 1-30 pm	J.S.
VILLERS CARBONELLES	3-3-18		Left VILLERS CARBONELLES 9-15 a.m., marched to VRAIGNES and arrived 11-30 am.	J.S.
VRAIGNES Location G.19.b.30	4-3-18		Sick animals admitted 23. Received & returned to Unit 1.	J.S.
"	5-3-18		2. Evacuated 22.	J.S.
"	6-3-18	"	1	J.S.
"	7-3-18	"	15	J.S.
"	8-3-18	"	5. Evacuated 18.	J.S.
"	9-3-18	"	18. Died 1.	J.S.
"	11-3-18	"	17. Received 6 returned to Unit 1.	J.S.
"	12-3-18	"	5. Evacuated 34. Died 1.	J.S.
"	13-3-18	"	41	J.S.
"	14-3-18	"	3. Evacuated 47.	J.S.
"	15-3-18	"	3	J.S.
"	16-3-18	"	8	J.S.

Army Form C. 2118.

WAR DIARY
INTELLIGENCE SUMMARY.

(Erase heading not required.)

Instructions regarding War Diaries and Intelligence Summaries are contained in F. S. Regs., Part II. and the Staff Manual respectively. Title pages will be prepared in manuscript.

Place	Date	Hour	Summary of Events and Information	Remarks and references to Appendices
VRAIGNES 43 Rue d'Brioni	17-3-18		Sick animals received & returned to Unit 1.	JS.
	18-3-18		admitted 39.	JS.
	19-3-18		4. Evacuated 61.	JS.
	20-3-18			JS.
	21-3-18		14. Discharged 1. Received & returned to Unit 3.	JS.
	22-3-18		12. Died 1. Discharged 12. Left VRAIGNES 1-0 pm, marched to DOINGT and arrived 8-0 pm.	JS.
DOINGT	23-3-18		Left DOINGT 1-0 am, marched to BIACHES and arrived 8-0 am.	JS.
BIACHES	24-3-18		Sick animals admitted 5. Left BIACHES 2-0 pm, marched to CAPPY and arrived 8-0 pm.	JS.
CAPPY	25-3-18		Left CAPPY 10-0 am, marched to BEAUVINCOURT and arrived 12-0 noon. Left BEAUVINCOURT 4-0 pm, marched to MERICOURT and arrived 9-0 pm.	JS.
MERICOURT	26-3-18		Left MERICOURT 9-0 am, marched to CERISY and arrived 11-0 am. Left CERISY 7-0 pm, marched to FOUILLOY and arrived 10-0 pm.	JS.
FOUILLOY	28-3-18		Sick animals received & returned to Unit 1. Left FOUILLOY 2-0 pm, marched to GENTELLES and arrived 5-0 pm. Left GENTELLES 6-0 pm, marched to CAGNY and arrived 11-0 pm.	JS.
CAGNY	30-3-18		Left CAGNY 3-0 pm, marched to SALOUEL and arrived 7-0 pm.	JS.

Army Form C. 2118.

WAR DIARY
INTELLIGENCE SUMMARY.

(Erase heading not required.)

Instructions regarding War Diaries and Intelligence Summaries are contained in F. S. Regs., Part II. and the Staff Manual respectively. Title pages will be prepared in manuscript.

Place	Date	Hour	Summary of Events and Information	Remarks and references to Appendices
SALOUEL	31-3-18		Left SALOUEL 2-0 p.m. marched to SEUX and arrived 6-0 p.m.	JS

J. Spruell Capt. A.V.C.T
Commanding Mobile Veterinary Section,
1/1 East Lancs.

WAR DIARY

of the

1/1 East Lancs Mobile Veterinary Section

From 1st April 1918   to   30th April 1918

(Volume: 14)

Army Form C. 2118.

WAR DIARY
or
INTELLIGENCE SUMMARY.
(Erase heading not required.)

Instructions regarding War Diaries and Intelligence Summaries are contained in F. S. Regs., Part II. and the Staff Manual respectively. Title pages will be prepared in manuscript.

Place	Date	Hour	Summary of Events and Information	Remarks and references to Appendices
SEUX Conteau 17 26.3.Y.	1-4-18		Sick horses admitted 2. Died 1.	J.S.
	2-4-18		" 3. Evacuated 17.	J.S.
LONG Hollinville 27.8.55	3-4-18		Left SEUX 2-0 pm. marched to GORENFLOS and arrived 10-0 pm.	J.S.
	4-4-18		Left LONG 9-0 am. marched to GORENFLOS and arrived 12-0 pm.	J.S.
BELLANCOURT	5-4-18		Left GORENFLOS 2-0 pm. marched to BELLANCOURT, and arrived 5-0 pm.	J.S.
Ailleville #4 ONEUX Ailleville 1 m 27. N.	6-4-18		Left BELLANCOURT 9-30 am. marched to ONEUX, and arrived 12-0 pm.	J.S.
	7-4-18		Sick horses admitted 4. Evacuated 4.	J.S.
	8-4-18		" Evacuated 5. Received & returned to Unit 1.	J.S.
	9-4-18		" admitted 4. Evacuated 5.	J.S.
	10-4-18		" 5. Evacuated 3.	J.S.
	11-4-18		" 6. Evacuated 8.	J.S.
	12-4-18		" 3. " 3.	J.S.
	13-4-18		" 3. " 5.	J.S.
	14-4-18		" 1. Evacuated 6.	J.S.
	15-4-18		" 1.	J.S.
	16-4-18		" 7.	J.S.

Army Form C. 2118.

WAR DIARY
INTELLIGENCE SUMMARY.
(Erase heading not required.)

Instructions regarding War Diaries and Intelligence Summaries are contained in F. S. Regs., Part II. and the Staff Manual respectively. Title pages will be prepared in manuscript.

Place	Date	Hour	Summary of Events and Information	Remarks and references to Appendices
ONEUX Abbeville 14. 26.7.17	17-4-18		Sick animals evacuated 5.	J.S.
"	18-4-18		" " admitted 5.	J.S.
"	19-4-18		" " evacuated 6.	J.S.
"	20-4-18		" " " 4. 1. Received & returned to Unit 1.	J.S.
"	21-4-18		" " evacuated 2. Left ONEUX 2-30 p.m. marched to LONG, arrived 5-45 p.m.	J.S.
LONG Abbeville 14. 66.86.	22-4-18		Left LONG 6-0 a.m. marched to LONGPRE, and arrived 7-0 a.m. Entrained and left LONGPRE 10-0 a.m. arrived WIZERNES 6-30 p.m. detrained and marched to TILQUES, arrived 11-0 p.m.	J.S.
TILQUES Hazebrouck 1:9 103 5:85	24-4-18		Sick animals admitted 3.	J.S.
"	25-4-18		" " " 15. Evacuated 18.	J.S.
"	26-4-18		Left TILQUES 9-45 a.m. marched to VAL de LUMBRES and arrived 12-30 p.m.	J.S.
VAL de LUMBRES Hazebrouck 1:19 G.H. 2:52	29-4-18		Sick animals admitted 4.	J.S.
"	30-4-18		" " " 1. Evacuated 4.	J.S.

J. Farrell Lieut./Capt. A.V.C.T
Commanding Mobile Veterinary Section,
1/1 East Lancs.

Confidential

War Diary

of

1/1st East Lancashire Mobile
Veterinary Section.

From 1st May 1918   To. 31st May 1918.

Army Form C. 2118.

WAR DIARY
INTELLIGENCE SUMMARY.
(Erase heading not required.)

Instructions regarding War Diaries and Intelligence Summaries are contained in F. S. Regs., Part II. and the Staff Manual respectively. Title pages will be prepared in manuscript.

Place	Date	Hour	Summary of Events and Information	Remarks and references to Appendices
VAL de LUMBRES	1-5-18		Sick animals admitted 3 Evacuated 4. Received & returned to Unit 1. Left VAL de LUMBRES	J.S.
			2-30 p.m. marched to NIELLES les BLEQUIN, and arrived 5-30 p.m.	J.S.
NIELLES les BLEQUIN	2-5-18		Left NIELLES les BLEQUIN 5-15 p.m. marched to DESVRES and arrived 8-15 p.m.	J.S.
DESVRES	3-5-18		Entrained and left DESVRES 11-20 a.m. detrained and left NOYELLES 4-30 p.m. marched to OFFEUX	J.S.
			and arrived 8-0 p.m.	J.S.
OFFEUX	4-5-18		Sick animals admitted 2	J.S.
"	5-5-18		" " " 2	J.S.
"	6-5-18		" " Evacuated 3	J.S.
"	10-5-18		" " admitted 1	J.S.
"	11-5-18		" " " 3	J.S.
"	12-5-18		" " " 5	J.S.
"	13-5-18		" " Evacuated 6	J.S.
"	14-5-18		" " " 6	J.S.
"	15-5-18		" " Evacuated 11 Received & returned to Unit 1.	J.S.
"	16-5-18		" " Evacuated 5	J.S.
"	17-5-18		" " " 2	J.S.

Army Form C. 2118.

WAR DIARY
INTELLIGENCE SUMMARY.
(Erase heading not required.)

Instructions regarding War Diaries and Intelligence Summaries are contained in F. S. Regs., Part II. and the Staff Manual respectively. Title pages will be prepared in manuscript.

Place	Date	Hour	Summary of Events and Information	Remarks and references to Appendices
OFFEUX	18-5-18		Sick animals admitted 6. Evacuated 7.	J.S.
"	19-5-18		" 4	J.S.
"	20-5-18		" 4 Evacuated 6. Received & returned to Unit 2.	J.S.
"	21-5-18		" 5	J.S.
"	22-5-18		" 5 Received & returned to Unit 1.	J.S.
"	23-5-18		" 1 Evacuated 12. Received & returned to Unit 1.	J.S.
"	24-5-18		" 6. Evacuated 4.	J.S.
"	25-5-18		" 4. Evacuated 2.	J.S.
"	26-5-18		" 4 Received & returned to Unit 1.	J.S.
"	27-5-18		" 3 Evacuated 10. Received & returned to Unit 2.	J.S.
"	28-5-18		" 2 " 4	J.S.
"	29-5-18		" Nil.	J.S.
"	30-5-18		" 2. Died 1.	J.S.
"	31-5-18		" 2. Evacuated 3.	J.S.

WAR DIARY.
of the

1/1 East Lancs Mobile Veterinary Section

From 1st June 1918 to 30th June 1918

(Volume 16)

Army Form C. 2118.

WAR DIARY
or
INTELLIGENCE SUMMARY.
(Erase heading not required.)

Instructions regarding War Diaries and Intelligence Summaries are contained in F. S. Regs., Part II. and the Staff Manual respectively. Title pages will be prepared in manuscript.

Place	Date	Hour	Summary of Events and Information	Remarks and references to Appendices
OFFEUX	1-6-18		Sick animals evacuated 1	J.S.
	2-6-18		Sick Animals admitted 1	J.S.
	3-6-18		" " " 4	J.S.
	4-6-18		" " " 6, returned to Unit 1, Evacuated 3	J.S.
	5-6-18		" " " 3	J.S.
	6-6-18		" " " 7	J.S.
	7-6-18		" " " 1 Evacuated 9, returned to Unit 1	J.S.
	8-6-18		" " " 6 " 2	J.S.
	9-6-18		" " " 1	J.S.
	10-6-18		" " " 4	J.S.
	11-6-18		" " " 1 Evacuated 3	J.S.
	12-6-18		" " " 5 " 2 transferred to 36 Auxiliary H.V.S. 14	J.S.
	13-6-18		" " " evacuated 3	J.S.
	14-6-18		" " " admitted 5	J.S.
	15-6-18		" " " 8, returned to Unit 1	J.S.
	16-6-18		" " " 2 Died 1, Evacuated 4	J.S.

Army Form C. 2118.

WAR DIARY
or
INTELLIGENCE SUMMARY.
(Erase heading not required.)

Instructions regarding War Diaries and Intelligence Summaries are contained in F. S. Regs., Part II. and the Staff Manual respectively. Title pages will be prepared in manuscript.

Place	Date	Hour	Summary of Events and Information	Remarks and references to Appendices
OFFEUX	17/6/18		Admitted Sick animals 2	J.S.
	18/6/18		Sick animals returned to Units 2, Evacuated 2	J.S.
	19/6/18		Admitted Sick animals 5, Evacuated 4	J.S.
	20/6/18		Sick animals admitted 2	J.S.
	21/6/18		" " " 1, Evacuated 3	J.S.
			Left OFFEUX at 9.30 a.m. marched to MESNIL TROIS FOETUS and arrived 5.30 p.m.	J.S.
MESNIL TROIS FOETUS	22/6/18		Left MESNIL TROIS FOETUS at 9 a.m. and marched to BERNAVILLE and arrived 5 p.m.	J.S.
BERNAVILLE	24/6/18		Sick animals admitted 1, Evacuated 1	J.S.
	25/6/18		" " " 2	J.S.
	27/6/18		" " " 1, Evacuated 4	J.S.
	28/6/18		" " " returned to Unit 1	J.S.
	30/6/18		" " " admitted 1	J.S.

J. Snell Ball, A.V.C.
Commanding Mobile Veterinary Section,
1/1 East Lancs.

Confidential
War Diary
of
1/1st East Lancashire Mobile
Veterinary Section.

Volume 17.

July 1918.

Army Form C. 2118.

Volume 19

WAR DIARY
or
INTELLIGENCE SUMMARY.
(Erase heading not required.)

Instructions regarding War Diaries and Intelligence Summaries are contained in F. S. Regs., Part II. and the Staff Manual respectively. Title pages will be prepared in manuscript.

Place	Date	Hour	Summary of Events and Information	Remarks and references to Appendices
BERNAVILLE	2-7-18		Sick horse admitted 1	J.S.
"	3-7-18		" " " 1	J.S.
"	4-7-18		" " " 1	J.S.
"	5-7-18		" " " 1 Evacuated 1	J.S.
"	6-7-18		" " " 2	J.S.
"	8-7-18		Received & returned to Unit 2	J.S.
"	9-7-18		Evacuated 4	J.S.
"	11-7-18		Received & returned to Unit 1	J.S.
"	13-7-18		admitted 1	J.S.
"	16-7-18		Received & returned to Unit 1	J.S.
"	20-7-18		admitted 2	J.S.
"	22-7-18		Left BERNAVILLE 9 a.m. marched to CANDAS, entrained & left CANDAS 11.45 a.m. arrived at SERQUEUX, detrained & left SERQUEUX 7.15 p.m. marched to GAILLEFONTAINE and arrived 10-9 p.m.	J.S.
GAILLEFONTAINE	23-7-18		Left GAILLEFONTAINE 9 a.m. marched to ABANCOURT and arrived 12.30 p.m.	J.S.
ABANCOURT	24-7-18		[ABANCOURT 9 a.m. marched to GAILLEFONTAINE and arrived 12 noon	J.S.

Army Form C. 2118.

WAR DIARY
or
INTELLIGENCE SUMMARY.
(Erase heading not required.)

Instructions regarding War Diaries and Intelligence Summaries are contained in F. S. Regs., Part II. and the Staff Manual respectively. Title pages will be prepared in manuscript.

Place	Date	Hour	Summary of Events and Information	Remarks and references to Appendices
GAILLEFONTAINE	Feb 7.18		Sick horses admitted 1	J.S.
	22.2.18		" " " 10. evacuated 3.	J.S.
	30.7		" " evacuated 6	J.S.
	31.7.18		1 horse returned to Unit 1	J.S.
	1.8.18		Left GAILLEFONTAINE at 10 a.m. reached SERQUEUX and entrained 11.30 p	J.S.

[signature]
Commanding Moore Veterinary Section, A.V.C.
East Lancs.

WAR DIARY.

of the

1/1 East Lancs Mobile Veterinary Section

from 1st August 1918   to 31st August 1918

(Volume 18).

Army Form C. 2118.

WAR DIARY
INTELLIGENCE SUMMARY.
(Erase heading not required.)

Instructions regarding War Diaries and Intelligence Summaries are contained in F. S. Regs., Part II. and the Staff Manual respectively. Title pages will be prepared in manuscript.

Place	Date	Hour	Summary of Events and Information	Remarks and references to Appendices
SERQUES	1-8-18		Sick animals admitted 1 Evacuated 1	J.S.
"	2-8-18		3	J.S.
"	3-8-18		3 Evacuated 5	J.S.
"	4-8-18		1	J.S.
"	5-8-18		1 Evacuated 3	J.S.
"	6-8-18		1	J.S.
"	7-8-18		1 Evacuated 2	J.S.
"	8-8-18		2	J.S.
"	9-8-18		Evacuated 2	J.S.
"	10-8-18		admitted 2	J.S.
"	13-8-18		2 Evacuated 5	J.S.
"	14-8-18		1 do 2	J.S.
"	19-8-18		3	J.S.
"	20-8-18		1 evacuated 5	J.S.
"	22-8-18		1	J.S.
"	23-8-18		1 Assumed duty as acting D.A.D.V.S.	J.S.

Army Form C. 2118.

WAR DIARY
or
INTELLIGENCE SUMMARY.
(Erase heading not required.)

Instructions regarding War Diaries and Intelligence Summaries are contained in F. S. Regs., Part II, and the Staff Manual respectively. Title pages will be prepared in manuscript.

Place	Date	Hour	Summary of Events and Information	Remarks and references to Appendices
SERQUES	24-8-18		Sick animals admitted 1	J.S.
"	25-8-18		" 2	J.S.
"	26-8-18		" 3 Evacuated 6	J.S.

J. Snell Capt. A.V.C.
Commanding Mobile Veterinary Section,
1/1 East Lancs.

Confidential

War Diary

of

1/1st East Lancs Mobile Veterinary
Section.

From 1st Sept. 1918.   To:- 30th Sept. 1918.

Volume XIX.

Army Form C. 2118.

WAR DIARY
INTELLIGENCE SUMMARY.
(Erase heading not required.)

Place	Date	Hour	Summary of Events and Information		Remarks and references to Appendices
SERQUES	1-9-18		Sick horses admitted	2	JfS
"	2-9-18		" " "	2 Evacuated 4	JfS.
"	3-9-18		" " "	1 Evacuated 2	JfS
"	4-9-18		" " "	1 Evacuated 2	JfS
"	5-9-18		" " "	1	JfS
"	6-9-18		" " "	4 Evacuated 5. tuned acting as D.A.D.V.S.	PLA
"	9-9-18		" " "	2 do 1	P.L.A
"	10-9-18		" " "	1	P.L.A
"	11-9-18		" " "	2 Evacuated 1	P.L.A
"	12-9-18		" " "	3	P.L.A
"	13-9-18		" " "	1 Evacuated 6	P.L.A
"	14-9-18		" " "	1	P.L.A
"	15-9-18		" " "	1	P.L.A
"	16-9-18		" " " evacuated 2. Lyr SERQUES 11-30 am. marched to ABANCOURT and		P.L.A
"			arrived 4-30 p.m.		P.L.A
ABANCOURT	17-9-18		Sick animals admitted 2		P.L.A

Army Form C. 2118.

WAR DIARY
INTELLIGENCE SUMMARY.
(Erase heading not required.)

Place	Date	Hour	Summary of Events and Information	Remarks and references to Appendices
ABANCOURT	18-9-18		Sick animals admitted 3. Evacuated 1	Off
"	19-9-18		" evacuated 5	Off
"	20-9-18		Left ABANCOURT 10-30 a.m. marched to SERQUES, arrived 4-0 p.m. entrained and left 7-0 p.m.	Off
"	21-9-18		arrived PETITE HOUVIN 4-30 a.m. detrained 5-30 a.m. marched to LE CAUROY and arrived 9-30 a.m.	Off
LE CAUROY	23-9-18		Sick animals admitted 1	J.S.
"	24-9-18		" " " 2	J.S.
"	25-9-18		" " " 8. Evacuated 2	J.S.
"	26-9-18		" " evacuated 8	J.S.
"	27-9-18		Left LE CAUROY 8-0 a.m. marched to RAINCHEVAL and arrived 4-30 p.m.	J.S.
RAINCHEVAL	28-9-18		Left RAINCHEVAL 8-30 a.m. marched to CORBIE, and arrived 4-30 p.m.	J.S.
CORBIE	29-9-18		" CORBIE 1-0 p.m. marched to MURCOURT and arrived 4-30 p.m.	J.S.

Capt A.V.C.T
Commanding 11th Regiment Section.
1/ East Lancs.

Confidential

War Diary

of

1/1st E. Lancs. M.V.S.

From 1st Oct/18.   To: 31st Oct/18

Volume XX

Army Form C. 2118.

WAR DIARY
INTELLIGENCE SUMMARY.
(Erase heading not required.)

Instructions regarding War Diaries and Intelligence Summaries are contained in F. S. Regs., Part II. and the Staff Manual respectively. Title pages will be prepared in manuscript.

Place	Date	Hour	Summary of Events and Information	Remarks and references to Appendices
MORCOURT	1-10-18		Left MORCOURT 09.45, marched to MONTAUBAN and arrived 17.00.	J.S.
MONTAUBAN	4-10-18		Sick animals admitted 2. Evacuated 2. Left MONTAUBAN 09.00, marched to COMBLES and arrived 13.00.	J.S.
COMBLES	5-10-18		Left COMBLES 09.00 marched to RONSSOY and arrived 17.30.	J.S.
RONSSOY	7-10-18		Sick animals admitted 1.	J.S.
"	8-10-18	"	10.	J.S.
"	8-10-18	"	15. Evacuated 24. Left RONSSOY 16-30 marched to BELLE VIEW FARM	J.S.
			BEAUREVOIR and arrived 21-30.	J.S.
BEAUREVOIR	9-10-18		Left BELLE VIEW FARM 10-00 marched to AVELU and arrived 13-00. Sick horses admitted 2.	J.S.
		"	Sick animals evacuated 4.	J.S.
AVELU	11-10-18	"	Sick animals admitted 11.	J.S.
"	12-10-18	"	3. Left AVELU 14-00, marched to MARETZ and arrived 15-00.	J.S.
MARETZ	13-10-18	"	35	J.S.
	14-10-18	"	4. Evacuated 43. Destroyed 1.	J.S.
	15-10-18	"	34. do 2 do 1.	J.S.
	16-10-18	"	25 do 34 Received & returned to Units 1.	J.S.

Army Form C. 2118.

WAR DIARY
of
INTELLIGENCE SUMMARY.
(Erase heading not required.)

Instructions regarding War Diaries and Intelligence Summaries are contained in F. S. Regs., Part II. and the Staff Manual respectively. Title pages will be prepared in manuscript.

Place	Date	Hour	Summary of Events and Information	Remarks and references to Appendices
MARETZ	17-10-18		Sick animals admitted 18. Evacuated 22. Died 1.	J.S.
"	18-10-18		" do 16 destroyed 1.	J.S.
"	19-10-18		" 30. Received & returned to Unit 3.	J.S.
"	20-10-18		" evacuated 28. Left MARETZ 10-00. marched to SERAINE and arrived 11-30.	J.S.
SERAINE	21-10-18		" admitted 1	J.S.
"	22-10-18		" 4. Evacuated 1.	J.S.
"	23-10-18		" do 14.	J.S.
"	24-10-18		" evacuated 2.	J.S.
"	25-10-18		" admitted 3	J.S.
"	26-10-18		" " 2	J.S.
"	27-10-18		" Received & returned to Unit 1.	J.S.
"	29-10-18		" admitted 4. destroyed 1. died 1.	J.S.
"	30-10-18		" " 1. Evacuated 5.	J.S.
"	31-10-18		" " 3	J.S.

J.Truswell Capt. M.V.O.7
Commanding Mobile Veterinary Section,
1/ East Lancs.

Confidential

WAR DIARY
of the
1/1 East Lancs Mobile Veterinary Section

from 1st November 1918 to 30th November 1918

(Volume 21)

Army Form C. 2118.

WAR DIARY
or
INTELLIGENCE SUMMARY.
(Erase heading not required.)

Instructions regarding War Diaries and Intelligence Summaries are contained in F. S. Regs., Part II. and the Staff Manual respectively. Title pages will be prepared in manuscript.

Place	Date	Hour	Summary of Events and Information	Remarks and references to Appendices
SERAIN	1-11-18		Sick & rivals admitted 4. Evacuated 4. Apmed duties O/P A.D.M.S. 66th Division	J.S.
	2-11-18		" " " 5	J.S.
	3-11-18		Left SERAIN 09.30 marched to LE CATEAU, and arrived 13.00 Location LES ESSARTS FARM	J.S.
LE CATEAU	5-11-18		Sick & rivals admitted 1	J.S.
	6-11-18		Left LE CATEAU 09.30 marched to LANDRICIES, and	J.S.
			arrived 14.00. Location G 49.c.2.1. Sheet 57a	J.S.
LANDRICIES	9-11-18		Sick & rivals admitted 10. Evacuated 8 Left LANDRICIES 09.30 marched to	J.S.
			TAISNIERES, and arrived 15.00. Location I.7.K.3.0. Sheet 57a	J.S.
TAISNIERES	10-11-18		Left TAISNIERES 09.30 marched to DOMPIERRE and arrived 12.00 Location I.7.K.3.0. Sheet 57a	J.S.
			Sick & rivals admitted 13	J.S.
DOMPIERRE	11-11-18		Left DOMPIERRE 09.30 marched to SARS POTIERES and arrived at 13.00 Location	J.S.
	12-11-18		F.30.c.2.2. Sheet 57a.	J.S.
SARS POTIERES	13-11-18		Sick & wounded admitted 7 Relinquished duties O/P A.D.M.S. 66th Division	J.S.
	14-11-18		" 13 destroyed 1	J.S.
	15-11-18		" 12 Evacuated 32. Received & returned to Unit 3	J.S.
	16-11-18		" 6 Received & returned to Unit 2.	J.S.

WAR DIARY
or
INTELLIGENCE SUMMARY.
(Erase heading not required.)

Army Form C. 2118.

Place	Date	Hour	Summary of Events and Information	Remarks and references to Appendices
SARS POTIERS	17.11.18		Animals evacuated 17.	9.S.
"	19.11.18		Left SARS POTIERES 17.00. marched to SOLRE CHATEAU and arrived 18.00.	9.S.
SOLRE CHATEAU	20.11.18		Left SOLRE CHATEAU 09.00. marched to FROID CHAPELLE and arrived 17.00. Location 21 Bn L/35.	9.S.
FROID CHAPELLE	21.11.18		Sick animals admitted 1. Left FROID CHAPELLE 12.30. marched to PHILIPVILLE	9.S.
			arrived at 17.30. Location Rue de la gare & Rue du Moulin	9.S.
PHILIPVILLE	22.11.18		Sick animals admitted 2.	9.S.
"	23.11.18		" 2. Revived returned to Unit 1.	9.S.
"	24.11.18		Revived returned to Unit 2. Left PHILIPVILLE 08.40. marched to	9.S.
			MOVI SART and arrived 15.15. Billet No. 70.	9.S.

G. Revell - Capt A.V.C.T.

o/c 1/Eastern Mobile Veterinary Section

WAR DIARY
INTELLIGENCE SUMMARY.
(Erase heading not required.)

Army Form C. 2118.

Mob Vet. See Vol 23

Place	Date	Hour	Summary of Events and Information	Remarks and references to Appendices
WAULSORT	3-12-18		Sick animals admitted 5 evacuated 5.	J.S.
"	4-12-18		" " " 5	J.S.
"	5-12-18		" " " 1 evacuated 5	J.S.
"	9-12-18		" " " 3	J.S.
"	10-12-18		" " " 4 evacuated 7.	J.S.
"	11-12-18		" " " 1	J.S.
"	12-12-18		" " " 2	J.S.
"	14-12-18		" " " 1 evacuated 3. Left WAULSORT 08.30, marched to CINEY, and arrived 15.00. Billet No 101 Rue de Commerce	J.S.
CINEY	15-12-18		Sick animals admitted 4	J.S.
"	17-12-18		" " " 7	J.S.
"	18-12-18		" " " 2 Received & returned to Unit 1.	J.S.
"	19-12-18		" " " 8	J.S.
"	20-12-18		" " " 1	J.S.
"	22-12-18		" " " 3 destroyed 1	J.S.
"	23-12-18		" " " 17	J.S.

Army Form C. 2118.

WAR DIARY
INTELLIGENCE SUMMARY.
(Erase heading not required.)

Place	Date	Hour	Summary of Events and Information	Remarks and references to Appendices
LINES	24-12-18		Sick animals admitted 25. Evacuated 22. Received & returned to Unit 1	J.S.
"	25-12-18		" evacuated 22.	J.S.
"	26-12-18		" admitted 10. Evacuated 24.	J.S.
"	27-12-18		" " 24 " 16	J.S.
"	28-12-18		" " 10	J.S.
"	29-12-18		" " 6 evacuated 14	J.S.
"	30-12-18		" " 18 " 1	J.S.
"	31-12-18			

J.Spinell - Capt R.A.V.C.T
O/c "11 East Lancs Mobile Veterinary Section"

CONFIDENTIAL

WAR DIARY
of the

1/1 East Lancs Mobile
Veterinary Section

from 1st March 1918 to 31st May 1918

(Volume no. 22)

WAR DIARY or INTELLIGENCE SUMMARY

Army Form C. 2118.

1/1 E Lan Vety Sec

Place	Date	Hour	Summary of Events and Information	Remarks and references to Appendices
CINEY	1-1-19		Sick horses admitted 14	g.s.
"	2-1-19		" 8	g.s.
"	3-1-19		" 7 Evacuated 16 Received & returned to Unit 1	g.s.
"	4-1-19		" 11 " 47	g.s.
"	6-1-19		" 32	g.s.
"	7-1-19		" 4	g.s.
"	8-1-19		" 28	g.s.
"	9-1-19		" 10 Evacuated 30 Received & returned to Unit 1	g.s.
"	10-1-19		" 4	g.s.
"	12-1-19		" Received & returned to Unit 4	g.s.
"	13-1-19		" 2	g.s.
"	14-1-19		" 4	g.s.
"	15-1-19		" 12	g.s.
"	16-1-19		" 4	g.s.
"	17-1-19		" 10 Evacuated 43	g.s.
"	18-1-19		" 25 Destroyed 4	g.s.

Army Form C. 2118.

WAR DIARY
INTELLIGENCE SUMMARY.
(Erase heading not required.)

Instructions regarding War Diaries and Intelligence Summaries are contained in F.S. Regs., Part II. and the Staff Manual respectively. Title pages will be prepared in manuscript.

II

Place	Date	Hour	Summary of Events and Information	Remarks and references to Appendices
CINEY	19-1-19		Sick animals admitted 11	J.S.
"	20-1-19	"	" " " 7	J.S.
"	21-1-19	"	Evacuated 20. Received & returned to Unit 5.	J.S.
"	22-1-19	"	" do 13	J.S.
"	23-1-19	"	" " 14	J.S.
"	24-1-19	"	Evacuated 15. Destroyed 3. Received & returned to Unit 1.	J.S.
"	25-1-19	"	Destroyed 1 Received & returned to Unit 3	J.S.
"	26-1-19	"	Received & returned to Unit 12.	J.S.
"	27-1-19	"	Major B.G. Anderson R.A.V.C.T. assumed command of Unit vice Captain J. Sowell R.A.V.C.T. granted leave	P.U.K.
"	28-1-19	"	Sick animals admitted 7 Destroyed 2.	P.U.K.
"	29-1-19	"	" " " 5 Received & returned to Unit 6	P.U.K.
"	30-1-19	"	" " " 5 " " " " 1	P.U.K.
"	31-1-19	"	" " " 13	P.U.K.

R.G. Anderson Major R.A.V.C.T.
Commanding 3 Mobile Veterinary Section,
1/1 East Lancs.

CONFIDENTIAL.

WAR DIARY

of the

1/1 East Lancs Mobile Veterinary Section

From 1st Jany 1919 to 31st Jany 1919

(Volume 23)

Confidential
War Diary
of
1st/1st East Lancs. M.V.S.
66th Division.

From 1st. Feb. 1919 to 28th Feb. 1919.

Volume XXIV

Army Form C. 2118.

WAR DIARY
or
INTELLIGENCE SUMMARY.
(Erase heading not required.)

Instructions regarding War Diaries and Intelligence Summaries are contained in F. S. Regs., Part II. and the Staff Manual respectively. Title pages will be prepared in manuscript.

Place	Date	Hour	Summary of Events and Information	Remarks and references to Appendices
CINEY	Feb. 1		Admitted 2 horses 4 horses sold for Butchery	P.G.L
	" 2		" 5 " "	P.G.L
	" 3		" 9 " and 8 mules	P.G.L
	" 5		" 1 horse	P.G.L
	" 6		" 1 "	P.G.L
	" 8		" 13 horses + 1 mule Inoculated 22 horses and 6 mules	P.G.L
	" 9		" 2 " + 1 " , 1 horse sold for Butchery	P.G.L
	" 10		" 7 " " 1 horse + 1 mule " "	P.G.L
	" 11		" 7 " " +1 mule	P.G.L
	" 13		" 2 " " + 2 mules	144
	" 14		" 176 " , 4 horses + 1 mule sold for Butchery, 12 horses + 2 mules evacuated to A.V.H. Andennes PARYS	P.S.L
	" 15		149 horses sold "Z" Surplus	J.S.
	" 16		Admitted 134 horses Destroyed 1 horse	J.S.
	" 17		138 horses sold "Z" Surplus	J.S.
	" 18		Admitted 2 horses + 1 mule , 5 horses sold for Butchery	J.S.
	" 19		Admitted 99 animals, 1 mule sold for Butchery, 1 mule returned to Unit	J.S.

Army Form C. 2118.

WAR DIARY
or
INTELLIGENCE SUMMARY.
(Erase heading not required.)

Instructions regarding War Diaries and Intelligence Summaries are contained in F. S. Regs., Part II. and the Staff Manual respectively. Title pages will be prepared in manuscript.

Place	Date	Hour	Summary of Events and Information	Remarks and references to Appendices
CINEY	Feb 20		149 Animals sold "Z" Surplus	J.S.
"	21		144 " " " "	J.S.
"	22		Admitted 4 horses and 1 mule sold for Butchery	J.S.
"	23		Sold "Z" Surplus	J.S.
"	24		194 " admitted	J.S.
"	25		145 " Sold "Z" Surplus	J.S.
"			2 horses + 1 mule sold for Butchery	J.S.
"	26		109 Animals admitted 4 horses sold for Butchery	J.S.
"	27		104 " Sold "Z" surplus, 1 horse returned to Unit	J.S.
"	28		118 " admitted	J.S.

J. Smee Capt R.A.V.C.
Commanding Mobile Veterinary Section,
1st East Lancs.

Confidential
War Diary
of
1/2nd East Lancashire Mobile Veterinary
Section

Volume 25

From 1-3-19   To 31-3-19

ARMY FORM W 3715A

CERTIFICAT CONSTATANT L'ABSENCE DE TOUTE MALADIE CONTAGIEUSE.

Je certifie que l'animal dont le signalement est donné ci-dessous a été malleiné, qu'il n'est atteint d'aucune maladie contagieuse, et qu'il a été marqué au fer rouge, en ma présence, du signe de la réforme.

Classe de l'animal.	Couleur	Sexe.	Taille.	Marques particulières sur le corps.

Date de la vente.......................

................CAPT.R.A.V.C.T.

Les animaux vicieux sont déclarés tels au moment de la vente.

ARMY FORM W.3715 A.

CERTIFICAT CONSTATANT L'ABSENCE DE TOUTE MALADIE CONTAGIEUSE.

Classe de l'animal.	Couleur.	Sexe.	Taille.	Marques particulières sur le corps.

Date de la vente.......................

................CAPT.R.A.V.C.T.

Les animaux vicieux sont déclarés tels au moment de la vente.

WAR DIARY or INTELLIGENCE SUMMARY.

Army Form C. 2118.

(Erase heading not required.)

Place	Date	Hour	Summary of Events and Information	Remarks and references to Appendices
CINEY	1/3/19		Sold to Inhabitants 181 Animals	
	2/3/19		Admitted 8 Animals	A.2
	3/3/19		" 10 " 2 animals returned to Units	A.2
	4/3/19		" 131 " 93 Animals sold to Inhabitants, 3 animals sold to Butcher	A.2
	5/3/19		" 9 " 5 Animals returned to Units	A.2
	6/3/19		" 186 " 1 " " " " 132 Sold to Inhabitants 2 Sold to Butcher	A.2
	7/3/19		" 4 "	A.2
	8/3/19		" 5 " Sold to Inhabitants 2 animals sold to Butcher	A.2
	9/3/19		" 2 "	A.2
	10/3/19		" 34 " 2 Animals sold to Butcher	A.2
	11/3/19		" 2 " Evacuated 8 Animals No 10b. to Units	A.2
	12/3/19		" 2 " 48 " Sold to Inhabitants 1 evacuated sold to Units	A.2
	13/3/19		3 animals sold to Butcher	A.2
	14/3/19		5 " " " "	A.2
	15/3/19		Admitted 4 Animals	A.2

Army Form C. 2118.

WAR DIARY
or
INTELLIGENCE SUMMARY.
(Erase heading not required.)

Instructions regarding War Diaries and Intelligence Summaries are contained in F. S. Regs., Part II. and the Staff Manual respectively. Title pages will be prepared in manuscript.

Place	Date	Hour	Summary of Events and Information	Remarks and references to Appendices
CINEY	18/3/19		2 Animals sold to Butcher	A.1
	19/3/19		3 " " " "	A.2
	21/3/19		Evacuated 34 Animals	A.2
	22/3/19		Admitted 1 Animal. 1 Animal returned to Unit	A.2
	23/3/19		2 " 2 " " "	A.2
	24/3/19		2 Animals evacuated 9 "Y" horses sent to Base.	A.2
	25/3/19		2 " Sold to Butcher	A.2
	27/3/19		Admitted 1 Animal. 1 Animal Sold to Butcher	A.2
	28/3/19		" " 2 animals	A.2
	29/3/19		" " 2 " 1 Animal sold to Butcher 1 Animal returned to Unit	A.2
	30/3/19		" " 2 "	A.2
	31/3/19		1 Animal returned to Unit	A.2

W. Orrosl. Capt. A. A.V.C.
Commanding Mobile Veterinary Section,
East Lancs.

Confidential
War Diary of
1/1st East Lancs Mobile
Veterinary Section

April 1917

Volume 26

Army Form C. 2118.

WAR DIARY
or
INTELLIGENCE SUMMARY.
(Erase heading not required.)

Instructions regarding War Diaries and Intelligence Summaries are contained in F. S. Regs., Part II, and the Staff Manual respectively. Title pages will be prepared in manuscript.

Place	Date	Hour	Summary of Events and Information	Remarks and references to Appendices
CINEY	1/4/19		Sold to Butcher 2 horses and 1 mule	K2
"	3/4/19		Sold to Vint 1 mule	K2
"	6/4/19		Admitted 1 horse	K2
"	7/4/19		do 1 do	K2
"	8/4/19		Sold to Butcher 3 horses	K2
"	10/4/19		Sold to Vint 1 horse	K2
"	11/4/19		Admitted 1 horse	K2
"	12/4/19		Surrendered 1 horse	K2
"	14/4/19		Admitted 3 horses and 1 mule	K2
"	15/4/19		Surrendered 3 do 1 do	K2
"	20/4/19		Admitted 1 horse	K2
"	2/4/19		Sold to Butcher 1 horse	K2
"	24/4/19		Admitted 1 horse Sold to Butcher 1 horse, surrendered 1 mule	K2
"	23/4/19		1 mule	K2

Commanding Mobile Veterinary Section.
1/1 East Lancs.

Army Form C. 2118.

WAR DIARY
or
INTELLIGENCE SUMMARY.

(Erase heading not required.)

Instructions regarding War Diaries and Intelligence Summaries are contained in F. S. Regs., Part II. and the Staff Manual respectively. Title pages will be prepared in manuscript.

Place	Date	Hour	Summary of Events and Information	Remarks and references to Appendices
CINEY	1/4/19		Sold to Butcher 2 horses and 1 mule.	
	3/4/19		Retd to Unit 1 mule	
	5/4/19		Admitted 1 horse	
	7/4/19		do 1 do	
	8/4/19		Sold to Butcher 3 horses	
	9/4/19		Retd to Unit 1 horse	
	11/4/19		Admitted 1 horse	
	12/4/19		Evacuated 1 horse	
	14/4/19		Admitted 2 horses and 1 mule	
	15/4/19		Evacuated 2 do do 1 do	
	20/4/19		Admitted 1 horse	
	24/4/19		Sold to Butcher 1 horse	
	29/4/19		Admitted 1 horse. Sold to Butcher 1 horse. Evacuated 1 mule	
			1 mule	

Commanding Mobile Veterinary Section,
1/7 East Lancs.

..........Cash Account.
..........191...   ....(VETERINARY HOSPITAL)..............
Voucher No........   (REMOUNT DEPOT   )

RETURN OF HORSES and MULES authorized to be
sold by

War Office letter dated ......   No.........

No. of Lot	Remount Depot or Veterinary Hospital to which it belongs.	Colour	Sex	Age	Cause of unfitness for Military Service.	Names of Purchasers	Amount for which horse was sold. Frcs.	Remarks accounting for horses not sold etc.
1.								
2.								
3.								
4.								
5.								
6.								
7.								
8.								
9.								
10.								
11.								
12.								
13.								
14.								
15.								
16.								
17.								
18.								
19.								
20.								
21.								

TOTAL GROSS PROCEEDS
DEDUCT COMMISSION OF AUCTIONEER AT %

Francs   Auctione

I acknowledge to have received   I certify that I was
the sum of Frcs ____ for the sale   present at the sale by Public
of ____ cast horses, and the same will   Auction by ____ ____ of
be credited to the Public in the   the horses mentioned, at
____ Command Cash Account,   on the ____
for the month of ____ 191 .   and that the above statement
                                             is correct in every particular.
.... Command Paymaster.   (Officer who
.... 191..   (attended the sale.

                                             Dated at ____ this __ day
                                             of ____ 191 .

War Diary
of
1/1st East Lancs Mobile Veterinary
Section

Volume 27.

May 1919

Army Form C. 2118.

WAR DIARY
or
INTELLIGENCE SUMMARY.
(Erase heading not required.)

Instructions regarding War Diaries and Intelligence Summaries are contained in F. S. Regs., Part II. and the Staff Manual respectively. Title pages will be prepared in manuscript.

Place	Date	Hour	Summary of Events and Information	Remarks and references to Appendices
CINEY	5/5/19		Admitted 1 horse 1 mule sold to Butcher	
	6/5/19		1 horse sold to Butcher	
	9/5/19		Admitted 1 horse 1 horse sold to Butcher	
	10/5/19		Transferred to 11th Remount Squadron 4 horses	
	12/5/19		do do do 2 "	
	15/5/19		Cadre and Cadre stores and equipment handed to 66th Div Train Headquarters	

Warren Capt R.A.V.C.
Commanding Mobile Veterinary Section,
1/1 East Lancs.